D0768824

GEMS
NATURE'S JEWELS
PEARLS

By Sarah Machajewski

Gareth Stevens
PUBLISHING

Please visit our website, www.garethstevens.com. For a free color catalog of all our high-quality books, call toll free 1-800-542-2595 or fax 1-877-542-2596.

Library of Congress Cataloging-in-Publication Data

Machajewski, Sarah, author.
 Pearls / Sarah Machajewski.
    pages cm. — (Gems : nature's jewels)
 Includes bibliographical references and index.
 ISBN 978-1-4824-2868-1 (pbk.)
 ISBN 978-1-4824-2869-8 (6 pack)
 ISBN 978-1-4824-2870-4 (library binding)
 1. Pearls—Juvenile literature. 2. Cultured pearls—Juvenile literature. I. Title.
 TS755.P3M25 2016
 639.412—dc23

                                    2014048104

First Edition

Published in 2016 by
Gareth Stevens Publishing
111 East 14th Street, Suite 349
New York, NY 10003

Copyright © 2016 Gareth Stevens Publishing

Designer: Andrea Davison-Bartolotta
Editor: Kristen Rajczak

Photo credits: Cover, p. 1 © iStockphoto.com/cobalt; p. 5 gerhardp/Shutterstock.com; p. 7 (main) DEA/Photo 1/De Agostini/Getty Images; pp. 7 (inset), 21 (pearl coloring) Balonici/Shutterstock.com; p. 8 Dlrohrer2003/Wikimedia Commons; p. 9 Cancan Chu/Getty Images; p. 10 Robert Kirk/Getty Images; p. 11 Werner Forman/Getty Images; p. 12 DEA/M. Seemuller/De Agostini/Getty Images; p. 13 William Albert Allard/National Geographic/Getty Images; p. 15 Franco Banfi/Getty Images; p. 17 © iStockphoto.com/itakefotos4u; p. 18 CM Dixon/Print Collection/Getty Images; p. 19 Art Media/Print Collector/Getty Images; p. 21 (layers) tuulijumala/Shutterstock.com.

Printed in the United States of America

CPSIA compliance information: Batch #CS15GS: For further information contact Gareth Stevens, New York, New York at 1-800-542-2595.

Contents

What Are Pearls? 4

How Are Pearls Made? 6

Natural Pearls, Cultured Pearls 8

What Do Pearls Look Like? 10

Finding Pearls in the Wild 12

Making Pearls in a Lab 14

Pearl Jewelry 16

Pearls Throughout History 18

Pearls and People 20

Glossary 22

For More Information 23

Index 24

Words in the glossary appear in **bold** type the first time they are used in the text.

What Are Pearls?

You've likely seen many kinds of **jewelry**. It may have been made of beautiful gems, or stones from nature. Sometimes jewelry is made of gems that come from nature, but aren't stones. They're pearls.

Pearls are round, hard objects that are made inside the shell of an animal called a mollusk. This gemstone has been highly prized for thousands of years. It's even been called the "queen of gems"! Let's take a closer look at what makes pearls so special.

Be a Gem Genius!

Mollusks are the animal group that includes oysters, snails, and mussels. Oysters are the most famous for producing pearls.

This pearl may have a long journey from the shell to being worn on someone's ear, neck, or wrist!

How Are Pearls Made?

Pearls are made inside oysters. An oyster's hard shell keeps out anything that could hurt its soft body. However, sometimes tiny bits of matter floating in the sea get trapped inside the shell. This irritates, or bothers, the oyster.

The oyster responds by making **substances** to coat the bit of matter. It makes six-sided crystals and a **protein** that holds the crystals together. The two substances together are called nacre (NAY-kuhr). The nacre builds up in **layers** around the object.

Be a Gem Genius!

The inside of some mollusk shells is coated with nacre. Mother-of-pearl is another name for nacre.

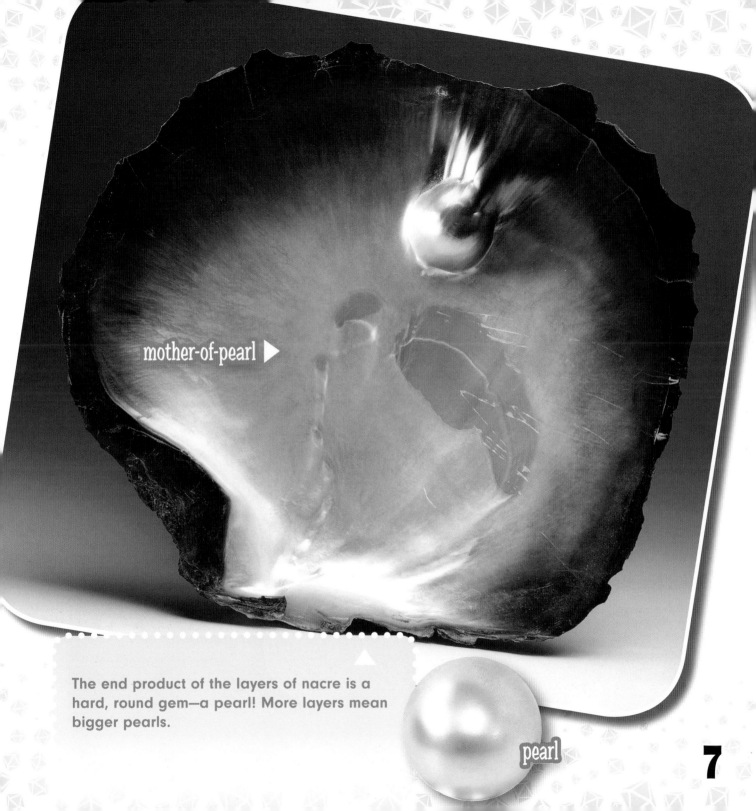

mother-of-pearl ▶

The end product of the layers of nacre is a hard, round gem—a pearl! More layers mean bigger pearls.

pearl

Natural Pearls, Cultured Pearls

Pearls are split into two groups based on how the pearl-making **process** starts. The groups are natural pearls and cultured pearls.

Natural pearls form when a tiny bit of matter gets stuck in an oyster's shell by accident, without any help from people. Cultured pearls form when people place something inside an oyster's shell on purpose. They know this will cause the oyster to release nacre and form a pearl. Natural pearls are **rare** and more costly than cultured pearls.

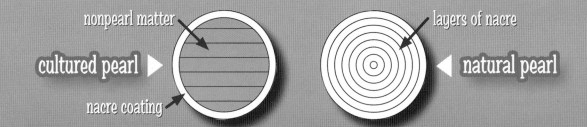

nonpearl matter

layers of nacre

cultured pearl ▶

◀ natural pearl

nacre coating

You can't tell if a pearl is natural or cultured just by looking at it. Gem experts can x-ray the pearl to look at the inside. Natural pearls have layers. Cultured pearls don't have any layers at all!

9

What Do Pearls Look Like?

When you look at a pearl, you may notice its color seems to change when you look at it from different angles. This is called iridescence (ihr-uh-DEHS-uhns). Iridescence is caused by luster, which is how a surface **reflects** light. Pearls are known for their high luster.

Pearls can be many shapes and colors. "Perfect" pearls are round, but oysters can make oval, semiround, flat, and baroque (teardrop-shaped) pearls, too. A perfect pearl has a clean surface. "Clean" means there are no cracks, bumps, holes, or scratches.

baroque pearl necklace

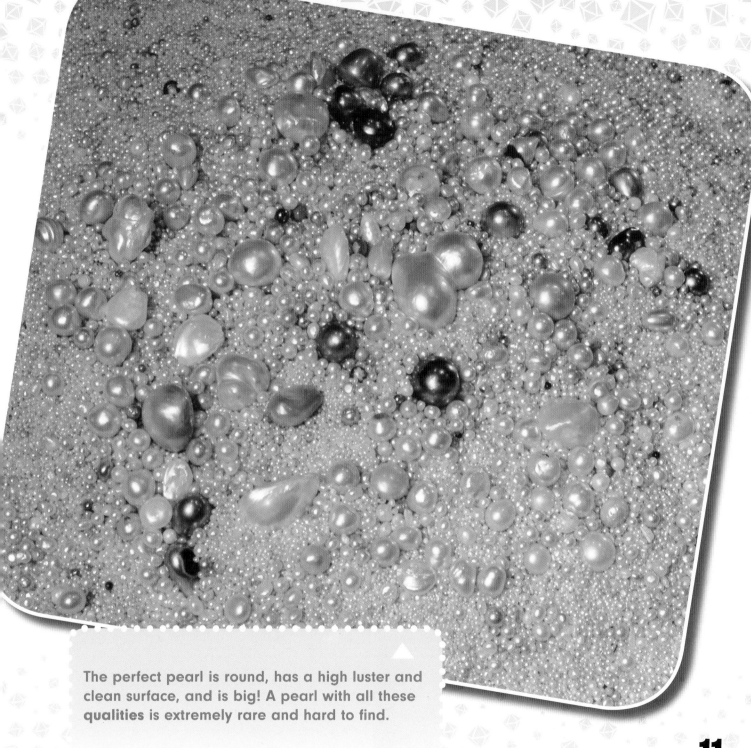

The perfect pearl is round, has a high luster and clean surface, and is big! A pearl with all these qualities is extremely rare and hard to find.

Finding Pearls in the Wild

People have searched the world's seas for pearls for thousands of years. The Persian Gulf, Red Sea, and coasts of India and Sri Lanka were once major oyster hot spots. Long ago, North America was considered the "land of pearls" because of the number of oysters living in its waters.

Diving was once the only way to find pearls. This was dangerous work, so it was often left to slaves or poor people. Some dove more than 100 feet (30 m) down!

People still dive for pearls today. They often have to hold their breath for a long time!

Making Pearls in a Lab

Long ago, finding pearls was dangerous—and a matter of luck. This changed around 1900, when two Japanese men separately learned how to culture a pearl. They put a tiny piece of metal or shell into an oyster's body. The oyster then produced a pearl sac that produced nacre, and finally, a pearl.

In 1916, a man named Kokichi Mikimoto created his own method for culturing round pearls. This was the beginning of the cultured pearl business, which changed the pearl industry forever.

Be a Gem Genius!

Oysters on pearl farms live on racks that are 30 to 50 feet (9 to 15 m) underwater. When their pearls are ready to be gathered, workers bring the racks to the surface-no diving necessary!

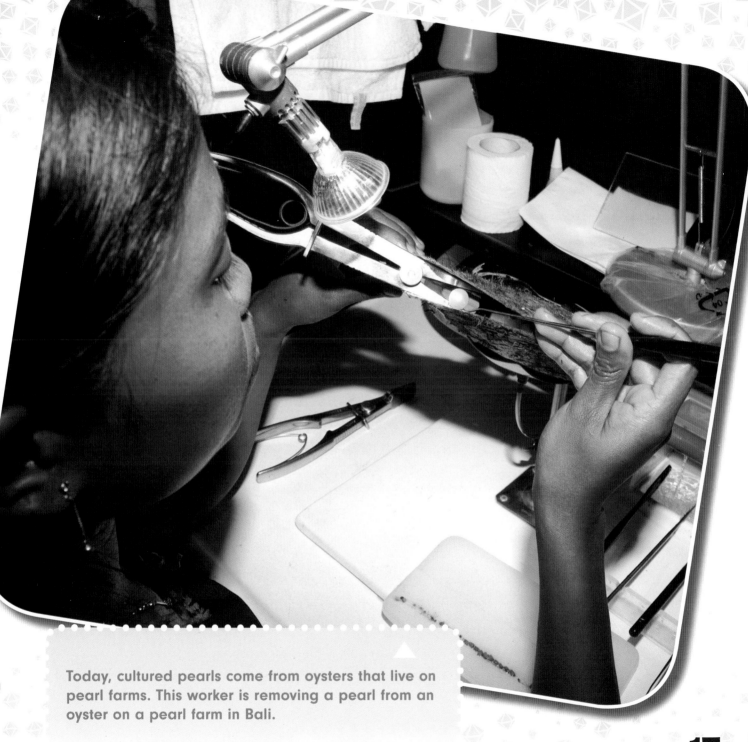

Today, cultured pearls come from oysters that live on pearl farms. This worker is removing a pearl from an oyster on a pearl farm in Bali.

Pearl Jewelry

Pearls are pretty to look at. They're also pretty to wear. The gem has been used to make some of the world's most beautiful jewelry. It can be made into earrings, necklaces, bracelets, and pins. Mother-of-pearl was once used to make buttons, combs, and more.

Pearls used to be very expensive because they were rare and hard to gather. This meant the gem was reserved for royalty. However, cultured pearls have made pearl jewelry much less expensive. Some people even wear fake pearls, which are made of plastic.

Be a Gem Genius!

You can tell the difference between a real pearl and fake pearl by biting it. If it feels gritty or rough, it's a real pearl!

Jewelry with real pearls can cost hundreds or thousands of dollars, depending on how many pearls are in it.

Pearls Throughout History

Pearls have played a big part throughout history. The ancient Romans were interested in pearls as early as the first century BC. Ancient Egyptians greatly valued pearls, too. According to stories, ancient Egyptian ruler Cleopatra once owned pearls that were worth over $9 million in today's money!

For many years, kings and queens have worn expensive pearl jewelry. European explorers in North America reported Native Americans wearing pearls for decoration. Pearls can be seen in famous art, such as the painting *Girl with a Pearl Earring*.

ancient Roman hair decoration ▶

Girl with a Pearl Earring was painted in 1665.

Pearls and People

People have been **fascinated** by pearls for what seems like forever. This may be because of their surprising origins. The iridescent gem hides under a bumpy, rough shell until someone is lucky enough to find it.

It's hard to imagine what the first person who opened an oyster and found a pearl must have thought. Since then, pearls have been a **symbol** of wealth and have become a major fashion statement. As long as oysters keep producing this beautiful gem, people will continue to love it.

Be a Gem Genius!

Some believe Julius Caesar took over land in Britain in 55 BC in order to find pearls.

Perfect Pearl Parts

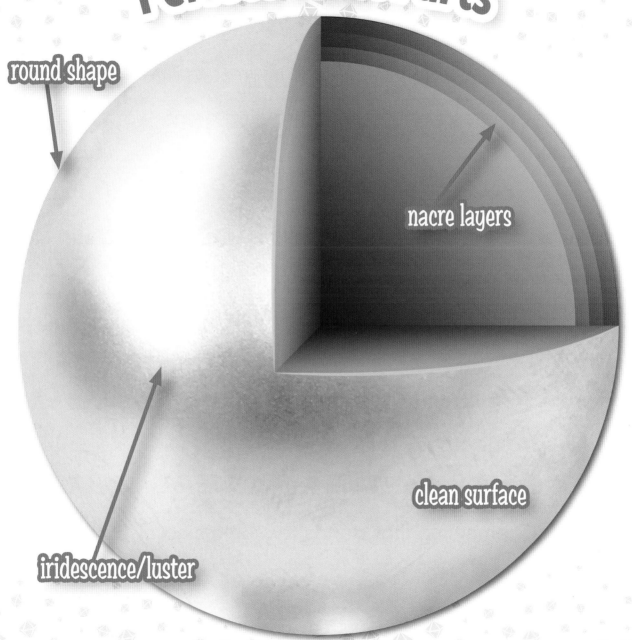

round shape

nacre layers

iridescence/luster

clean surface

Glossary

fascinate: to strongly command interest or attention

jewelry: pieces of metal, often holding gems, worn on the body

layer: one thickness lying over or under another

process: a series of steps or actions taken to complete something

protein: a necessary element found in all living things

quality: a feature

rare: not common

reflect: to give back light

substance: a certain kind of matter

symbol: something that stands for something else

For More Information

Books

Tomecek, Steve. *Everything Rocks and Minerals.* Washington, DC: National Geographic, 2010.

Zoehfeld, Kathleen Weidner. *Rocks and Minerals.* Washington, DC: National Geographic, 2012.

Websites

Gem Explorer
gemkids.gia.edu/view-all-gemstones
This interactive website provides a closer look at the world's most beautiful gems.

Gems
www.kidsgeo.com/geology-for-kids/0025A-gems.php
This website teaches readers all about gems.

Index

color 10

cultured pearls 8, 9, 14, 15, 16

diving 12, 13, 14

Egyptians 18

fake pearls 16

India 12

iridescence 10, 20

jewelry 4, 16, 17, 18

layers 6, 7, 9

luster 10, 11

Mikimoto, Kokichi 14

mollusk 4, 6

mother-of-pearl 6, 16

nacre 6, 7, 8, 14

Native Americans 18

natural pearls 8, 9

North America 12, 18

oysters 4, 6, 8, 10, 12, 14, 15, 20

pearl farms 14, 15

perfect pearl 10, 11

Persian Gulf 12

Red Sea 12

Romans 18

shapes 10

shell 4, 5, 6, 8, 20

Sri Lanka 12

surface 10, 11